D1568792

Freedom of
SPEECH
Should There Be Limits?

Bradley Steffens

ReferencePoint
Press®

San Diego, CA

About the Author

Bradley Steffens is a novelist, a poet, and an award-winning author
of more than sixty nonfiction books for children and young adults.

© 2024 ReferencePoint Press, Inc.
Printed in the United States

For more information, contact:
ReferencePoint Press, Inc.
PO Box 27779
San Diego, CA 92198
www.ReferencePointPress.com

ALL RIGHTS RESERVED.
No part of this work covered by the copyright hereon may be reproduced or used in any form or by any
means—graphic, electronic, or mechanical, including photocopying, recording, taping, web distribution,
or information storage retrieval systems—without the written permission of the publisher.

Picture Credits:
Cover: Eyeidea/Shutterstock.com

6: Reuters/Alamy Stock Photo
9: AC NewsPhoto/Alamy Stock Photo
11: Historical Images Archive/Alamy Stock Photo
14: Rawpixel.com/Shutterstock.com
18: goodluz/Shutterstock.com
20: Associated Press
24: Africa Studio/Shutterstock.com

28: Jinitzail Hernandez/Shutterstock.com
32: Reuters/Alamy Stock Photo
34: Ringo Chiu/Shutterstock.com
39: Associated Press
43: bgrocker/Shutterstock.com
46: ZUMA Pess, Inc./Alamy Stock Photo
49: American Photo Archive/Alamy Stock Photo
51: ©Look and Learn/Bridgeman Images
54: E Ozcan/Shutterstock.com

LIBRARY OF CONGRESS CATALOGING-IN-PUBLICATION DATA

Names: Steffens, Bradley, 1955- author.
Title: Freedom of speech : should there be limits? / by Bradley Steffens.
Description: San Diego, CA : ReferencePoint Press, Inc., 2023. | Includes
    bibliographical references and index.
Identifiers: LCCN 2023001017 (print) | LCCN 2023001018 (ebook) | ISBN
    9781678205768 (library binding) | ISBN 9781678205775 (ebook)
Subjects: LCSH: Freedom of speech--United States--Juvenile literature
Classification: LCC KF4772 .S735 2023 (print) | LCC KF4772 (ebook) | DDC
    342.7308/53--dc23/eng/20230403
LC record available at https://lccn.loc.gov/2023001017
LC ebook record available at https://lccn.loc.gov/2023001018

Contents

Meeting the Challenge of Toxic Expression

On December 27, 2022, the Ninth Circuit Court of Appeals ruled that the Albany Unified School District in Albany, California had not violated the free speech rights of two students when it expelled them for posting racist words and images on Instagram that in some cases featured Black classmates. The two students had sued the school district, claiming that the First Amendment to the Constitution, which states that "Congress shall make no law . . . abridging the freedom of speech, or of the press," protected them from punishment by the state. They further asserted that they made the posts on a private, invitation-only account, on their own time, and not while in school. The court disagreed. "We hold that, under the circumstances of this case, the school properly disciplined two of the involved students for bullying," wrote Judge Daniel Collins for the unanimous court. "Students . . . remain free to express offensive and other unpopular viewpoints, but that does not include a license to disseminate severely harassing invective targeted at particular classmates in a manner that is readily and foreseeably transmissible to those students."[1]

A Flood of Harmful Speech

The facts in the Albany Unified School District Case illustrate a growing problem—that social media makes it easy for bad actors to spread hateful expression at speeds and volumes never seen before. Facebook reported that it had identified and removed 28.6 million hate speech posts in the first half of 2022, an increase of 472 percent from the same period in 2018. Twitter banned, suspended, or otherwise penalized more than 1 million different accounts from July to December 2020 for violating its hate speech policy, a 77 percent increase over the prior six-month period.

Hate speech is not the only harmful expression being spread via the internet. Social media is also being swamped by false and misleading information. A June 2022 survey by the research firm Statista found that 43 percent of North American social media users reported seeing false or misleading information about politics in the week prior to the survey. The spread of intentionally false information, known as disinformation, is having a devastating effect on the trust people have in their governments and elections. "Major democratic institutions . . . have correctly identified fake news as a threat to their values and processes, but the real danger lurks in the corrosive effect that these online lies have on citizens' trust in their democracy," says Merten Reglitz, a senior lecturer at the University of Birmingham in the United Kingdom. "Fake news leads to a loss of trust of citizens in each other—a major cause of destabilising democratic processes."[2]

Limits on Governmental Action Against Speech

Under the First Amendment, there is little the US government can do to limit false information. The only time the government gets involved with false statements is when they are made to officials investigating a crime, made to defraud people for money, or designed to harm a person's reputation. In the 2012 case *United States v. Alvarez*, the Supreme Court stated:

> Absent from those few categories where the law allows content-based regulation of speech is any general exception to the First Amendment for false statements. This comports with the common understanding that some false statements are inevitable if there is to be an open and vigorous expression of views in public and private conversation, expression the First Amendment seeks to guarantee.[3]

According to the free speech tradition rooted in the First Amendment, the proper response to false speech is not to suppress it but to allow other speech to expose its errors, leading peo-

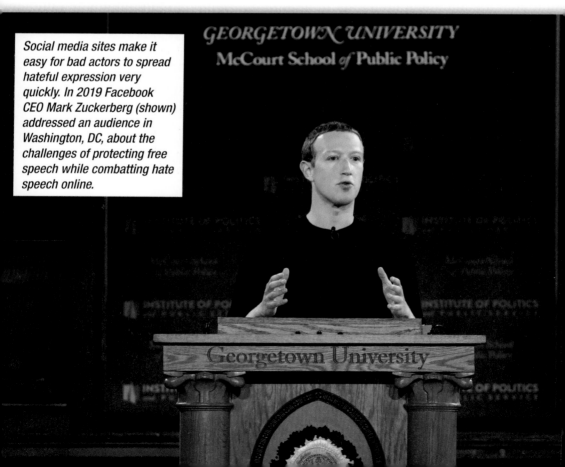

Social media sites make it easy for bad actors to spread hateful expression very quickly. In 2019 Facebook CEO Mark Zuckerberg (shown) addressed an audience in Washington, DC, about the challenges of protecting free speech while combatting hate speech online.

ple to reject it. "The remedy for speech that is false is speech that is true," wrote Justice Anthony Kennedy for the majority in *United States v. Alvarez*. "The response to the unreasoned is the rational; to the uninformed, the enlightened; to the straight-out lie, the simple truth."[4]

"The remedy for speech that is false is speech that is true."[4]

—Anthony Kennedy, Supreme Court justice

Doubts About the Free Speech Model

A growing number of scholars are questioning whether the traditional model of countering bad speech with better speech can meet the challenges of a digital society replete with software designed to overwhelm social media with harmful expression. David Pozen, a law professor at Columbia Law School, writes:

> We have no basis in evidence or experience to predict that increasing the quality or quantity of true speech on the internet will reliably neutralize false speech or inculcate true beliefs in society. For those ends, measures that seek to limit the salience and spread of false speech— whether by prioritizing authoritative news sources, downranking or removing deceptive content, or imposing penalties on serial purveyors of harmful lies—may well be more effective.[5]

Using technology to combat harmful speech presents its own set of problems. While artificial intelligence can be used to locate and remove disfavored speech, it is human beings who must set the parameters for which speech to suppress. Since human opinions are not neutral, there will always be claims that these parameters are unjustly influenced by politics, belief systems, and self-interest. In such circumstances, it can be difficult to determine objective truth and to easily separate harmful speech from speech that is useful and true.

The Doctrine of Free Speech

In December 2022 journalists Matt Taibbi and Bari Weiss began publishing memos, emails, messages, and other documents revealing steps that executives within Twitter had taken to suppress news stories and commentary posted by certain Twitter users. The tweets were suppressed not because they violated any rules or policies but because they expressed viewpoints that the Twitter executives believed to be harmful. These internal documents showed that the Twitter executives used a kind of software known as visibility filtering to remove disfavored tweets from hashtag searches, prevent them from appearing on the app's trending page, and block searches of their authors. "Think about visibility filtering as being a way for us to suppress what people see to different levels," a senior Twitter employee told Weiss. "It's a very powerful tool."[6]

Taibbi and Weiss received the internal Twitter files from Elon Musk, the new chief executive officer (CEO) of Twitter, as part of his plan to bring transparency to the social media giant, which he purchased in October 2022. Musk and others had long suspected that Twitter had been manipulating the popular social media platform to silence particular voices. As Twitter's single largest shareholder, Musk had urged the company to reveal details about its content-moderation practices. When it refused, Musk—then the richest person in the world—bought the company, vowing to end its practice of suppressing speakers and viewpoints. "The reason I acquired Twitter is because it is important to the future of civilization to have a common digital town square, where a wide range of beliefs can be debated in a healthy manner, without resorting to violence," Musk wrote in an open letter to Twitter advertisers. "I didn't do it to make more money. I did it to try to help humanity, whom I love."[7]

> "The reason I acquired Twitter is because it is important to the future of civilization to have a common digital town square, where a wide range of beliefs can be debated in a healthy manner, without resorting to violence."[7]
>
> —Elon Musk, Twitter CEO

The Counterspeech Doctrine

A self-described free speech absolutist, Musk subscribes to the theory that all speech, except for speech forbidden by law, should be allowed in public debate. This includes speech that some people—or even most people—believe to be false, hurtful,

Elon Musk purchased Twitter in 2022. Previously, he had long suspected that Twitter had been manipulating the social media platform to silence particular voices. As the new owner, he vowed to bring greater transparency to the social media site.

or offensive. This theory, known as the counterspeech doctrine, does not suggest that there is no such thing as harmful speech. It recognizes that such speech not only exists but is far too common. But the counterspeech doctrine holds that the best way to deal with harmful speech is not to suppress it but to engage with it—to counter bad speech with good speech and to expose false ideas with true ones. As Justice Louis D. Brandeis put it in his concurring opinion in the Supreme Court case *Whitney v. California* (1927), "If there be time to expose through discussion, the falsehoods and fallacies, to avert the evil by the processes of education, the remedy to be applied is more speech, not enforced silence."[8]

The counterspeech doctrine has its roots in a 1644 speech and pamphlet titled *Areopagitica* by the English poet and essayist John Milton. At the time of Milton's speech, the English Parliament required publishers to submit manuscripts for review prior to publication. If the content was approved, the publisher could print it. However, if the manuscript contained views judged to be harmful or untrue, the publishers would not be allowed to print the work. The practice of preventing publication of works based on their content is known as prior restraint.

The problem with prior restraint, as Milton saw it, was that humanity's judgment was imperfect. Putting a small group of people in charge of deciding what the public could read was unwise, because even in the best of circumstances the reviewers would make mistakes, and the public would be deprived of valuable insights and information. In more worrisome circumstances, the reviewers could suppress what the monarchy or other powerful leaders wanted suppressed.

Milton argued that a better approach to managing public discourse would be to allow publishers to print whatever they believed to be worthwhile and allow readers to decide for themselves what is good and bad, true and false. Milton believed that if

> "If there be time to expose through discussion, the falsehoods and fallacies, to avert the evil by the processes of education, the remedy to be applied is more speech, not enforced silence."[8]
>
> —Louis D. Brandeis, Supreme Court justice

The counterspeech doctrine has its roots in the speech (and later pamphlet) titled Areopagitica *that was written by the English poet and essayist John Milton, pictured here.*

all ideas were allowed to compete on equal terms, good ideas would triumph over bad ones. "Let [Truth] and Falsehood grapple," Milton wrote. "Who ever knew Truth put to the worse, in a free and open encounter. Her confuting is the best and surest suppressing."[9]

The counterspeech doctrine supports the rights not only of speakers and publishers but also of hearers and readers. It recognizes the right of individuals to be exposed to all ideas, arguments, and opinions and to make up their own minds about issues. Milton found this right to be the most important of all human rights. "Give me the liberty to know, to utter, and to argue freely according to conscience, above all liberties,"[10] he wrote.

Milton's arguments persuaded the public and Parliament that prior restraint was a bad policy, and in 1695 Parliament did not renew the law that enabled it. Prior restraint ended, but this did not mean that the press was completely free. Writers and publishers could still be held responsible for injuries caused by their words. In his 1765 book *Commentaries on the Laws of England*, English jurist William Blackstone explained the limits of a free press:

> The liberty of the press is indeed essential to the nature of a free state; but this consists in laying no previous restraints upon publications, and not in freedom from censure for criminal matter when published. Every freeman has an undoubted right to lay what sentiments he pleases before the public; to forbid this, is to destroy the freedom of the press: but if he publishes what is improper, mischievous, or illegal, he must take the consequences of his own temerity.[11]

Constitutional Guarantees of Free Speech

The newly independent English colonists in North America adopted this model of free expression and incorporated it into the Constitution of the United States. The First Amendment to the US Constitution reads, in part, "Congress shall make no law . . . abridging the freedom of speech, or of the press." The Fourteenth Amendment extends that prohibition to state and local governments. In short, the First Amendment prevents government officials from suppressing expression before it occurs or punishing it afterward, unless it breaks a law or violates another person's legally protected rights.

Although the words of the Constitution are clear, the document is not "self-defining and self-enforcing,"[12] as Justice Felix Frankfurter once put it. People must interpret how it applies in differing situations. Judges at various levels of the government can decide free speech issues, but Article 3 of the Constitution makes the Supreme Court the final arbiter of the Constitution's meaning.

Exceptions to First Amendment Protection

Some Supreme Court justices have argued that the First Amendment means exactly what it says, with no exceptions. One of these justices was Hugo Black. "Madison and the other Framers of the First Amendment, able men that they were, wrote in language they earnestly believed could never be misunderstood: 'Congress shall make no law . . . abridging freedom . . . of the press,'"[13] wrote Black in his concurring opinion in *New York Times Co. v. United States* (1971). In his concurring opinion in *Smith v. California* (1959), Black was even more blunt: "I read 'no law . . . abridging' to mean *no law abridging*."[14] Black and other free speech absolutists believe that counterspeech is the only check on negative speech permitted by the Constitution.

The Supreme Court as a whole has never embraced the absolutist position. As Justice Henry Billings Brown explained in *Robertson v. Baldwin* (1897):

The law is perfectly well settled that the first ten amendments to the Constitution, commonly known as the "Bill of Rights," were not intended to lay down any novel principles of government, but simply to embody certain guaranties and immunities which we had inherited from our English ancestors, and which had, from time immemorial, been subject to certain well recognized exceptions arising from the necessities of the case.[15]

Over the years, the Supreme Court has defined seven exceptions to the general rule that the government cannot limit or punish speech. These categories of speech include defamation (harming a person's reputation based on false claims), false and

Do Presidents Have an Unlimited Right of Free Speech?

Catherine J. Ross, a constitutional law professor at George Washington University, suggests that the public employee legal doctrine can be used to punish presidents for lying. In *Garcetti v. Ceballos* (2006), the Supreme Court ruled that speech by a public employee is not protected by the First Amendment when the statements are part of the speaker's routine duties. Ross suggests that this standard can be applied to presidents and that they could be removed from office for making false statements as part of their job. She writes:

Is there any way to stop a president who lies constantly about matters large and small, who regularly displays his disconnection from facts or verifiable reality, and whose lies endanger the nation and threaten the very foundations of democracy? . . .

I propose a novel approach drawn from an obscure corner of First Amendment jurisprudence: the public employee speech doctrine. Under that analysis, presidents should have less right to lie than the rest of us because all public employees surrender some of their free speech rights as a condition of employment and also because the unique amplification of the president's falsehoods has unparalleled power to harm.

Catherine J. Ross. *A Right To Lie?* Philadelphia: University of Pennsylvania Press, 2021.

A woman uses social media while she rides the subway. Critics argue that bad actors can use fake accounts to overwhelm social media with false information, making it impossible to counter each false post with a true one.

deceptive advertising (which defrauds the public), incitement (urging and convincing people to break the law), fighting words (speech that is likely to provoke an immediate and violent reaction), obscenity (sexually explicit material that has no social or literary value), child pornography (sexually explicit material that uses or simulates the use of underage models or actors), and a compelling interest of the government (material that undermines the government's ability to protect public health and safety, especially in matters of national security and war).

The Marketplace of Ideas

Outside of these exceptions to First Amendment protections, the Supreme Court has said that society must rely on the counter-speech doctrine to combat negative speech. The court has suggested that public debate works like an economic market in which bad products and services are driven out by better ones. "The best test of truth is the power of the thought to get itself accepted in the competition of the market,"[16] wrote Justice Oliver Wendell

Holmes Jr. in his dissent in *Abrams v. United States* (1919). In *United States v. Rumely* (1953), Justice William O. Douglas described the competition of thoughts pressing for acceptance as occurring in a "market place of ideas."[17] Since then, the "marketplace of ideas" has become "a powerful idea, underpinning much of First Amendment jurisprudence," writes David Schultz, a professor at Hamline University in St. Paul, Minnesota. "It remains perhaps the most pervasive metaphor to justify broad protections for free speech."[18] For example, Justice Stephen Breyer used the term in his concurring opinion in *Reed v. Town of Gilbert* (2015), writing that "whenever government disfavors one kind of speech, it places that speech at a disadvantage, potentially interfering with the free marketplace of ideas."[19]

Recently, critics of the counterspeech doctrine have argued that the internet is making the marketplace of ideas obsolete. They argue that bad actors can use fake social media accounts

Criticizing the Marketplace of Ideas

John Naughton, a professor at the Open University in Milton Keynes, England, doubts that the marketplace of ideas is an effective—or even real—antidote to harmful speech. He is especially critical of Elon Musk's reliance on the marketplace of ideas to moderate content on Twitter:

> Underpinning Musk's views about free speech and the public sphere (AKA town square) is the fatuous metaphor of "the marketplace of ideas" that emerged from the deliberations of the US supreme court in 1953 (though something like it was mooted by Justice Oliver Wendell Holmes way back in 1919). It suggests that ideas compete with each other in a conceptual marketplace where they can be critically evaluated by every individual. As law professor David Pozen and others have pointed out, there's no empirical evidence that a larger volume of speech, or a more open "marketplace" of ideas, tends to lead people away from falsity and towards truth. Subscribing to the metaphor is thus either a matter of faith or of evidence-free credulity. And if Musk believes that it is the secret sauce for managing Twitter then he's a bigger crackpot than even I thought.

John Naughton, "Elon Musk Needs to Learn That More Debate Does Not Mean More Truth," *The Guardian* (Manchester, UK), November 19, 2022. www.theguardian.com.

"On the web, it's not enough to battle falsehood with truth. The truth doesn't always win. In the age of social media, the marketplace model doesn't work."[20]

—Richard Stengel, author, editor, and former government official

and posting software, known as bots, to overwhelm social media with false information, making it impossible to counter each false post with a true one. "On the web, it's not enough to battle falsehood with truth," writes Richard Stengel, a former editor of *Time* and former US Department of State undersecretary for public diplomacy and public affairs. "The truth doesn't always win. In the age of social media, the marketplace model doesn't work."[20]

Private Companies and Limits on Speech

As a private company, Twitter is not governed by the First Amendment, which applies only to actions taken by government bodies and officials. Because they are not bound by the First Amendment, many private entities have enacted speech codes that prohibit speech that would otherwise be protected, including offensive language, sexually explicit material, and hate speech. Since social media platforms—including Twitter, Facebook, TikTok, and YouTube—are owned and operated by private companies, they are allowed to limit speech.

However, private companies can adopt First Amendment free speech standards if they wish to, and that seems to be Musk's intention. "By 'free speech,' I simply mean that which matches the law," Musk explained in a tweet. "I am against censorship that goes far beyond the law. If people want less free speech, they will ask government to pass laws to that effect. Therefore, going beyond the law is contrary to the will of the people."[21] As highly respected as the counterspeech doctrine is, and as well as it has worked in the past to expose bad ideas and promote good ones, it is unclear whether it will continue to serve the public in the future.

CHAPTER TWO

Free Speech on Campus

In the fall of 2021, following the COVID-19 school shutdowns, the library at Daniel Pearl Magnet High School in Los Angeles remained closed even after the school reopened. Students working on the school newspaper learned that the library was closed because the librarian had not gotten the COVID-19 vaccine, as required by the school district, and was therefore not allowed to return to work. The student journalists wrote an article about the situation, referring to the librarian by name and giving the reason for her absence. Believing that her privacy rights were being violated, the librarian complained, and the school principal demanded that the librarian's name be removed from the article. When the students, backed by their faculty advisor, Adriana Chavira, refused to comply with the demand, the school district moved to suspend Chavira for three days and put a disciplinary note in her employment file.

The students and Chavira turned to the Student Press Law Center in Washington, DC, for help. The organization mounted an appeal of Chavira's suspension, arguing that the school district's action violated the constitutional rights of Chavira and her students. After a lengthy appeal, the disciplinary action was rescinded on September 16, 2022. Hadar Harris, the executive director of the Student Press Law Center, says:

This is something that goes on across the country all the time. Student journalists do really important work, reporting newsworthy stories in their schools and in their communities all the time. And the fact that they don't have protections—and even where they do, they're not applied correctly—is really problematic, speaks to freedom of the press, speaks to trying to ensure that young people can use their voice and ask critical questions and speaks really to the future and health of our democracy.[22]

First Amendment Protections in Schools

The Student Press Law Center based its appeal on a landmark Supreme Court case that extended First Amendment protections to both students and teachers. In *Tinker v. Des Moines Independent Community School District* (1969), the high court ruled that public school officials cannot suppress student expression unless it will disrupt school activities or infringe on the rights of others. Nevertheless, speech inside schools is not as free as speech in the rest of society. This is because the government has a compelling in-

Student journalists work together on a project. Student journalists often find themselves in situations where there is disagreement over how far their free speech rights extend.

terest in maintaining a school environment that is orderly and conducive to learning. As a result, schools retain the right to restrict speech related to classwork, including the preparation of school newspapers in journalism classes. However, such limits do not encompass all speech, especially speech with political content. Restrictions must be narrowly tailored to maintaining order and promoting educational goals.

"It can hardly be argued that either students or teachers shed their constitutional rights to freedom of speech or expression at the schoolhouse gate."[23]

—Abe Fortas, Supreme Court justice

The *Tinker* case arose in December 1965, when thirteen-year-old Mary Beth Tinker, her fifteen-year-old brother John Tinker, and their sixteen-year-old friend Christopher Eckhardt faced suspension for wearing black armbands to school to protest the Vietnam War. Two federal courts sided with the school district, agreeing that the school's rule against wearing armbands was a reasonable way to keep order and to promote learning. The Supreme Court disagreed. "First Amendment rights, applied in light of the special characteristics of the school environment, are available to teachers and students," wrote Justice Abe Fortas for the majority. "It can hardly be argued that either students or teachers shed their constitutional rights to freedom of speech or expression at the schoolhouse gate."[23]

Fortas laid out what has become known as the *Tinker* standard, a guideline for when school officials are allowed to restrict student expression. According to the Supreme Court, censorship can only occur when school authorities can "reasonably . . . forecast substantial disruption of or material interference with school activities." That was not the case with the wearing of armbands by the students in the *Tinker* case. Fortas wrote:

These petitioners merely went about their ordained rounds in school. . . . They neither interrupted school activities nor sought to intrude in the school affairs or the lives of others. They caused discussion outside of the classrooms, but no interference with work and no disorder. In the circumstances, our Constitution does not permit officials of the State to deny their form of expression.[24]

Misuse of the Tinker Standard

The *Tinker* standard has helped schools maintain order, but it has also been used against students in ways that violate their right to free speech. In January 2018 an eighteen-year-old student named Addison Barnes, a senior at Liberty High School in Salem, Oregon, was sent home for wearing a controversial shirt to a class that was scheduled to discuss immigration policies. The shirt was emblazoned with a logo for a fictitious firm, the "Donald J. Trump Border Wall Construction Co.," a reference to then-president Trump's construction of a steel barrier on parts of the US border with Mexico. Barnes was told that one student and one teacher had complained about the shirt. He was given the option of covering up the shirt or going home. At first, he complied, wearing a jacket over the shirt, but in the afternoon he took off the jacket. He was sent home for displaying his shirt's message.

Liberty High School had been the site of recent sit-ins and demonstrations against Trump's border policy. Referring to these incidents, the Hillsboro School District used the *Tinker*

In this 2013 photo, sixty-one-year-old Mary Beth Tinker holds a photo of herself and her brother, John Tinker, from when she was suspended from school at thirteen for protesting the Vietnam War. The picture shows the black arm bands they wore. Tinker took her case to the Supreme Court.

standard to justify the school's actions. "Liberty High School administration believed they could reasonably forecast that Mr. Barnes' shirt might cause other students to feel unsafe and could potentially lead to walkouts, altercations, or other disruptive actions," explained the school district. School administrators "acted out of an abundance of caution on behalf of the student body to ensure safety."[25]

Barnes sued the school district in federal court, arguing that his First Amendment right to free speech had been violated. US district judge Michael W. Mosman agreed. He issued a temporary restraining order, stopping the school from suspending Barnes or banning the shirt. "There's not enough to go on here to show that sort of legitimate concern justifying censorship of this core political speech,"[26] Mosman declared. Lawyers for Barnes and the school district eventually settled the lawsuit. Under the settlement, the principal was required to write an apology to Barnes, and the school district had to pay the student $25,000 for attorneys' fees.

No Protection for Promoting Illegal Drugs

As Mosman's ruling suggests, political speech is more protected than other speech, especially in a school setting. Political speech receives special protection under the First Amendment because of the role it plays in shaping elections and, through them, the governance of the nation. Social commentary is also vital to democracy, but it does not receive the same level of protection as political speech, especially in a school situation. For example, in a 2007 case known as *Morse v. Frederick*, the Supreme Court found that a message promoting the use of marijuana could be prohibited in a school setting because it challenged the school's antidrug policies, even though the message contained some social commentary.

In *Morse v. Frederick*, Joseph Frederick, an eighteen-year-old student at Juneau-Douglas High School in Alaska, unfurled a 14-foot (4.3 m) banner with the message "Bong Hits 4 Jesus" in front of television cameras as the 2002 Winter Olympics torch

A Victory for Academic Free Speech

For a lesson on argumentative writing, a professor from San Diego Mesa College (SDMC) wrote a sample thesis statement on the board of a college-level English course for seniors at San Diego's Madison High School in September 2022. The statement read, "As it is currently constituted, the Republican Party is now a fascist organization that no longer fits the category of a conventional Democratic Party." After receiving complaints from students and parents, SDMC launched an investigation of the professor. The Foundation for Individual Rights and Expression (FIRE) wrote a letter to the college president, protesting the investigation. The letter states in part:

> As a public institution of higher education, SDMC is bound by the First Amendment. . . .
>
> Absent the protections afforded by the First Amendment, college courses open to high school students or young college students would be subject to paternalistic censorship, chilling faculty members' ability to select materials and tailor discussions to best serve their pedagogical [teaching] interests. If left to stand, such restrictions could easily be abused, chilling the ability of college instructors to discuss any divisive topic, including those of race, sex, and gender.
>
> On October 12, 2022, the college announced that it would not discipline the professor.

Foundation for Individual Rights and Expression, "FIRE Letter to San Diego Mesa College, September 29, 2022," September 29, 2022. www.thefire.org.

relay passed near his school—a sanctioned off-campus school event. The principal of Juneau-Douglas High School, Deborah Morse, who was standing nearby, confiscated the banner and ordered Frederick to her office. Writing for the majority, Chief Justice John Roberts explained that Morse's action was justified in the school context. He wrote:

> When Frederick suddenly and unexpectedly unfurled his banner, Morse had to decide to act—or not act—on the spot. It was reasonable for her to conclude that the banner promoted illegal drug use—in violation of established school policy—and that failing to act would send a power-

ful message to the students in her charge, including Frederick, about how serious the school was about the dangers of illegal drug use.[27]

Roberts reasoned that whatever social message was contained in the banner did not save it from suppression. "We discern no meaningful distinction between celebrating illegal drug use in the midst of fellow students and outright advocacy or promotion,"[28] he wrote.

Justice Samuel Alito agreed with the majority decision, with the understanding that the ruling is limited to "speech that a reasonable observer would interpret as advocating illegal drug use." In his concurring opinion, Alito emphasized that social commentary, even about marijuana, is protected in a school setting. He wrote, "I join the opinion of the Court on the understanding that . . . it provides no support for any restriction of speech that can plausibly be interpreted as commenting on any political or social issue, including speech on issues such as 'the wisdom of the war on drugs or of legalizing marijuana for medicinal use.'"[29]

> "We discern no meaningful distinction between celebrating illegal drug use in the midst of fellow students and outright advocacy or promotion."[28]
>
> —John Roberts, chief justice of the US Supreme Court

Limits on Teachers

Like students, teachers at federally funded schools do not enjoy full free speech rights on campus, especially in terms of social commentary. However, the burden is on the school to show that the limits on speech are necessary to achieving its academic goals. In 2016 a federal appeals court found that Lincoln Brown, a sixth-grade teacher in Chicago, could be disciplined for using the N-word in a classroom setting, even though he was leading a discussion on why it was wrong to use racial slurs.

A middle school teacher lectures his students. Teachers at federally funded schools face free speech limits in terms of what they can and cannot say to students.

Brown had intercepted a note being passed in class that contained bullying language and read part of the note aloud to illustrate why it was intimidating. The classroom discussion turned to the use of demeaning language. The school principal happened to visit the class during the discussion and heard Brown use the N-word while explaining its hurtful nature. Since the school district has a policy against using that word in any context, the school board moved to suspend Brown for five days without pay.

Brown challenged the suspension in federal court, maintaining that his First Amendment rights had been violated. The US District Court for the Northern District of Illinois sided with the school district, and a federal appeals court upheld the decision. The courts found that the Chicago Public Schools policy against using the word was clear and narrowly tailored to advance academic goals, and therefore Brown's claim of First Amendment protection was not valid under the law.

Protecting Off-Campus Speech

The ability of schools to limit offensive speech is not strictly limited to words spoken on campus or even at school-sponsored events. In a 2021 case, the Supreme Court explained that the *Tinker* standard covers off-campus speech that involves bullying or harassment targeting particular individuals, threats aimed at teachers or other students, and the failure to follow rules concerning schoolwork and participation in online school activities. However, in that case, *Mahanoy Area School District v. B.L.*, the court ruled that schools do not have the ability to limit off-campus political speech or social commentary, no matter how crude and offensive it might be.

The *Mahanoy* case involved two Snapchat messages taken and posted after school by Brandi Levy, a sophomore at Mahanoy Area High School in Mahanoy City, Pennsylvania. Disappointed

An Argument to Protect Student Speech

Writing for the majority in *Mahanoy Area School District v. B.L.* (2021), Supreme Court justice Stephen Breyer took a moment to remind school officials of the importance of protecting unpopular speech, no matter how crudely it may be expressed. He explained:

> The school itself has an interest in protecting a student's unpopular expression, especially when the expression takes place off campus. America's public schools are the nurseries of democracy. Our representative democracy only works if we protect the "marketplace of ideas." This free exchange facilitates an informed public opinion, which, when transmitted to lawmakers, helps produce laws that reflect the People's will. That protection must include the protection of unpopular ideas, for popular ideas have less need for protection. Thus, schools have a strong interest in ensuring that future generations understand the workings in practice of the well-known aphorism, "I disapprove of what you say, but I will defend to the death your right to say it."

Mahanoy Area School District v. B.L., 594 U.S. ___ (2021).

at failing to make the school's varsity cheerleading squad, Levy posted a photograph of herself and a friend making a vulgar gesture with the caption (fully spelled out) "F--- school f--- softball f--- cheer f--- everything."[30] When school officials saw the image and caption, they suspended Levy from the cheerleading team for a year for violating school rules. Levy apologized, but the school's athletic director, principal, superintendent, and school board all affirmed the suspension.

Levy took her case to a federal district court, and the court found that the school's punishment violated the student's First Amendment rights. The school district appealed to the US Court of Appeals for the Third Circuit, which upheld the district court's ruling, finding that the circumstances allowing schools to regulate on-campus speech do not apply to off-campus speech. The school district then appealed to the Supreme Court. The high court voted 8–1 to uphold the lower court rulings, but it disagreed with the Third Circuit's sweeping finding about off-campus speech. "Unlike the Third Circuit, we do not believe the special characteristics that give schools additional license to regulate student speech always disappear when a school regulates speech that takes place off campus," wrote Justice Stephen Breyer for the majority. However, schools cannot regulate "all the speech a student utters during the full 24-hour day."[31] This is especially true of political, religious, or social commentary. Although Levy's criticism of the school's cheer program was crudely worded, it did contain some social criticism.

As court rulings have shown, the First Amendment's protections of the right to free speech extend to both students and teachers, but those rights are not as full as the rights of most other Americans. The need for schools to maintain a safe environment and promote academic goals means that they can limit speech that might otherwise be protected, including profanity, the promotion of drug use, and hate speech.

CHAPTER THREE

False and Misleading Information

In September 2022 four members of the media research firm NewsGuard typed search terms into the popular social media app TikTok. Each time they conducted a search, the analysts used a new account so the search results would not reflect any previous activity on the platform. In all, the researchers analyzed 540 TikTok search results, looking at the top twenty results from twenty-seven searches on news topics. The terms they searched covered a range of topics—the Russia-Ukraine war, the 2022 US midterm elections, COVID-19, abortion, and school shootings. Sometimes they tried less-specific search terms, including "2022 election" and "mRNA vaccine." Other times they used more controversial terms, including "January 6 FBI" and "Uvalde tx conspiracy." The results helped paint a picture of the app's search algorithm.

Spreading False Information on TikTok

What the researchers found shocked them. Almost one-fifth (19.4 percent) of the top-ranking videos contained false or misleading information. "TikTok . . . repeatedly delivered videos containing false claims in the first 20 results, often within the first five," wrote the researchers. "Google, by comparison, provided higher-quality and less-polarizing results, with far less misinformation."[32] The results are important, because in 2021 TikTok surpassed Google as the most popular website worldwide, according to the internet content delivery company Cloudflare.

One of the most disturbing findings the researchers made was that when they typed a more generalized term into the search bar, the app automatically suggested searches for terms leading to false and misleading content. For example, when a NewsGuard analyst searched for "Uvalde," seeking information about the May 2022 shooting at Robb Elementary School in Uvalde, Texas, which left nineteen children and two teachers dead, the first result suggested by the TikTok search bar was "Uvalde tx conspiracy." Similarly, when a researcher typed in the term "climate change," the search bar suggested searches for "climate change debunked" and "climate change doesn't exist." A search

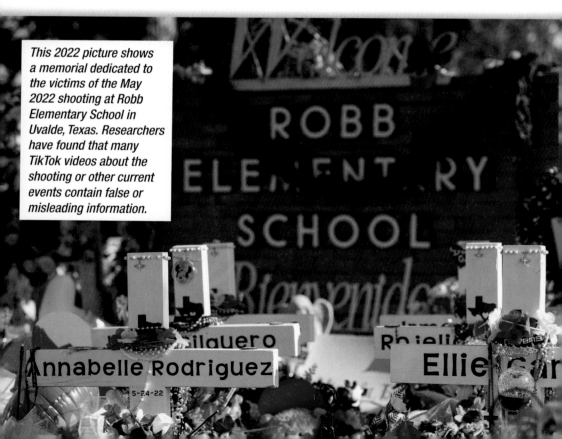

This 2022 picture shows a memorial dedicated to the victims of the May 2022 shooting at Robb Elementary School in Uvalde, Texas. Researchers have found that many TikTok videos about the shooting or other current events contain false or misleading information.

for "covid vaccine" generated suggestions for "covid vaccine injury," "covid vaccine truths," "covid vaccine exposed," "covid vaccine hiv," and "covid vaccine warning."[33]

TikTok is just one of countless repositories of false and misleading information. NewsGuard reports that in 2020, there were 16.3 billion engagements with news sources on social media worldwide. Of these, an astonishing 2.8 billion, or 17 percent of the total, came from unreliable sources. The number of engagements with unreliable sources was four times greater in 2020 than it was in 2019.

Misinformation, Disinformation, and Malinformation

False and misleading information can be categorized as misinformation, disinformation, or malinformation. Misinformation is false information that people spread unintentionally. Disinformation is false information spread intentionally. Malinformation is factual information that bad actors share, typically out of context, to serve a harmful purpose. Confusingly, these terms are sometimes used interchangeably.

Misinformation is inevitable. Well-meaning people often spread information they believe is helpful without knowing it is false. During the COVID-19 pandemic, for example, people passed along tips, advice, and home remedies for the illness that they sincerely believed in but that were not based on scientific facts. Their intentions were not to harm but to help.

The same false information that is spread as misinformation can also be disinformation, if the person sharing it has bad intentions. In fact, much of the misinformation spread by well-meaning people during COVID-19 originated from people who wanted to cast doubt on government policies and the medical establishment. They made urgent warnings to avoid vaccinations and masks as a way of thwarting public policy. In such cases the false information is categorized as disinformation.

While a great deal of disinformation and malinformation is spread to advance a specific cause, much of it has a less-focused purpose. It is designed to sow doubts and confusion and, by doing so, to erode confidence in existing institutions. Jamais Cascio, distinguished fellow at the Institute for the Future, explains:

> The power and diversity of very low-cost technologies allowing unsophisticated users to create believable "alternative facts" is increasing rapidly. It's important to note that the goal of these tools is not necessarily to create consistent and believable alternative facts, but to create plausible levels of doubt in actual facts. The crisis we face about "truth" and reliable facts is predicated less on the ability to get people to believe the "wrong" thing as it is on the ability to get people to "doubt" the right thing.

Quoted in Science, Technology & the Future, *Jamais Cascio—Are 'Alternative Facts' Created to Be Believed, or to Cast Doubt on Reality?*, YouTube, November 27, 2020. https://youtu.be/F8gRfw2d_ls.

People spread disinformation for many reasons. Sometimes their motives are political. They hope that the false information they share will influence people's opinions or even their votes. They know the information they are sharing is false or misleading, but they feel justified in spreading it because they believe that their political party or candidate is good and the opposition bad. The same thinking is sometimes adopted by people dedicated to a cause that they believe is not gaining the popularity it deserves—whether it is animal rights, climate change, gun control, or legalized abortion. For them, the higher moral purpose justifies their actions.

When the information presented is factual but the context is misleading, the message is deemed to be malinformation. For example, gun control advocates often say that roughly one hundred Americans lose their lives every day due to gun violence. This information is true, but it lacks context. Over 60 percent of US gun-related deaths are suicides. If guns were not available, people who are determined to end their own lives would likely do so using other means. By lumping suicides in with gang violence, police shootings, workplace violence, and domestic violence, the gun control advocates portray society as almost three times more violent than it really is. This malinformation gives their cause greater urgency, which can lead to greater acceptance of their proposed solution.

Protections for False Information

Despite the very real dangers that misinformation, disinformation, and malinformation pose to society, there is almost nothing the government can do about it. When the Supreme Court has considered cases involving false and misleading information, it has specifically said that such speech is protected by the First Amendment, unless it is aimed at an individual or is used to commit fraud. "Erroneous statement is inevitable in free debate," wrote Justice William Brennan in *New York Times Co. v. Sullivan* (1964), "and . . . it must be protected if the freedoms of expression are to have the 'breathing space' that they 'need . . . to survive.'"[34] In his opinion, Brennan referred to the high court's earlier finding in *Cantwell v. State of Connecticut* (1940):

> "Erroneous statement is inevitable in free debate, and . . . it must be protected if the freedoms of expression are to have the 'breathing space' that they 'need . . . to survive.'"[34]
>
> —William Brennan, Supreme Court justice

To persuade others to his own point of view, the pleader, as we know, at times, resorts to exaggeration, . . . and even to false statement. But the people of this nation have ordained in the light of history, that, in spite of the probability of excesses and abuses, these liberties are, in the long view, essential to enlightened opinion and right conduct on the part of the citizens of a democracy.[35]

Defamation and False Advertising

The two exceptions to First Amendment protection for false speech involve defamation (spreading false information about a person with the intent of harming that person's reputation) and false and deceptive advertising. In the case of defamation, the government allows lawsuits to go forward and for courts to award damages to punish the harmful speech. In the case of false and deceptive advertising, people can sue for damages they incurred because of the deceptive practices. The government can also charge the false advertisers with fraud and related crimes.

Defamation takes two forms: slander, which is spoken, and libel, which is printed or otherwise published. To prevail in court, litigants must show that the information being spread about them is false and caused real harm, such as lost income. If a statement causes harm to a person's reputation but the accusation is true, the person spreading the information cannot be sued for defamation. The information must be both harmful and false.

To protect the free flow of information in the realm of government and politics, the Supreme Court has set a higher standard for proving the defamation of public officials and public figures. In *New York Times Co. v. Sullivan* (1964), the court said that public figures must prove not only that the information about them is false but also that the speaker or writer acted with "actual

Members of the US Supreme Court pose for a photo in 2022. The court has specifically said that false and misleading information is protected by the First Amendment unless it is aimed at an individual or is used to commit fraud.

malice"—that is, the speaker knew the information was false or acted "with reckless disregard of whether it was false or not."[36] Proving actual malice requires finding a witness, an email, or some other evidence that the person spreading the information knew ahead of time that it was false.

While the protections of the First Amendment are sweeping, the high court has found that individuals have the right to protect their reputation, even if it punishes some speech. In *Rosenblatt v. Baer* (1966), Justice Potter Stewart explained that the ability to sue for defamation "reflects no more than our basic concept of the essential dignity and worth of every human being—a concept at the root of any decent system of ordered liberty."[37]

Suppressing False Information in Social Media

Today the majority of false and misleading information is spread via the internet, especially through social media. While the government itself cannot censor or punish the spread of false information, social media companies can and do. All the major social media platforms have policies against spreading false and misleading information, and they enforce these policies with a combination of artificial intelligence and human review.

In May 2022 Meta, which owns Facebook and Instagram, reported that from the beginning of the COVID-19 pandemic to June 2021, the company had displayed warnings on more than 190 million pieces of content that its third-party fact-checking partners rated as false, partly false, altered, or missing content. Meta also acts against political posts that have been found to be false by fact-checkers, posts from untrusted news publishers, and behavior that artificially boosts engagement or views, such as the use of bots and fake accounts. Meta reports that from October to December 2021, its artificial intelligence software detected and removed 1.7 billion fake accounts, often within minutes of registration.

Pressuring Private Companies to Censor Speech

While the government cannot suppress speech in social media itself, it can ask and even pressure social media companies to do so. Elon Musk released internal documents, known as the Twitter Files, in which the Trump administration and the Biden administration separately asked Twitter to suppress hundreds of tweets and suspend dozens of accounts for spreading what the officials called false information about COVID-19 policies. Sometimes the pressure was intense. Twitter's head of US public policy, Lauren Culbertson, wrote that the Biden administration was "not satisfied with Twitter's enforcement approach as they wanted Twitter to do more and to de-platform several accounts. Because of this dissatisfaction, we were asked to join other calls. They were very angry in nature."[38] When Musk learned that the government was pressuring Twitter to suppress speech, he tweeted, "If this isn't a violation of the Constitution's First Amendment, what is?"[39]

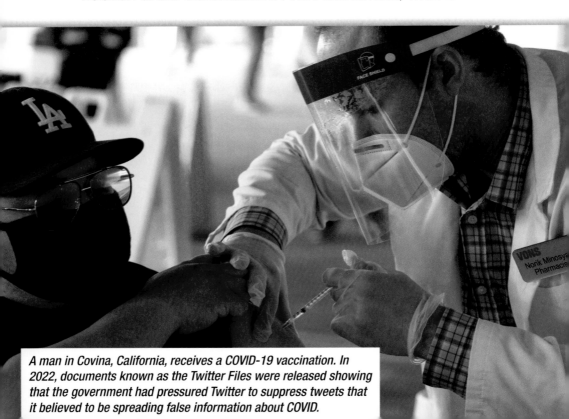

A man in Covina, California, receives a COVID-19 vaccination. In 2022, documents known as the Twitter Files were released showing that the government had pressured Twitter to suppress tweets that it believed to be spreading false information about COVID.

Based on the Twitter Files released through December 2022, the government's actions did not violate the First Amendment. According to the Supreme Court, the government can advise and even pressure private companies to suppress speech. What it cannot do is coerce a private company into suppressing speech by threatening it. The line between pressure and coercion was drawn in a case known as *Bantam Books, Inc. v. Sullivan* (1963). In this case, the Rhode Island state legislature created a commission that notified book distributors that certain publications were unfit for sale or display to minors. The commission warned distributors that the list of objectionable publications had been circulated to local police departments with a recommendation to prosecute the sellers of the materials. As a result of these notices, the largest book distributor in Rhode Island stopped filling orders for books and magazines on the commission's list.

> "The Commission deliberately set about to achieve the suppression of publications deemed 'objectionable,' and succeeded in its aim. . . . Their operation was in fact a scheme of state censorship effectuated by extra-legal sanctions; they acted as an agency not to advise but to suppress."[40]
>
> —William Brennan, Supreme Court justice

Four publishers with books on the commission's list went to court, arguing that the commission's practices violated the First Amendment. The Supreme Court agreed. Justice William Brennan wrote for the majority:

It is true that . . . books have not been seized or banned by the State, and that no one has been prosecuted for their possession or sale. But . . . the record amply demonstrates that the Commission deliberately set about to achieve the suppression of publications deemed "objectionable," and succeeded in its aim. . . . Their operation was in fact a scheme of state censorship effectuated by extra-legal sanctions; they acted as an agency not to advise but to suppress.[40]

As *Bantam Books, Inc. v. Sullivan* makes clear, a private company's actions can violate the First Amendment if it takes those actions because of threats from the government. In the Twitter Files case, it does not appear that the government's pressure rose to the level of threats and coercion. The Twitter team appeared to be happy to cooperate with the government. The same is true for Meta. In testimony before Congress, Meta CEO Mark Zuckerberg admitted that the social media companies do not adhere to the same standards of free speech that the First Amendment requires of the government. "Sometimes the right thing to do from a safety or security perspective isn't the best for privacy or free expression, so we have to choose what we believe is best for our community and for the world,"[41] said Zuckerberg.

Suing to Protect a Reputation

On November 13, 2022, four University of Idaho students—Kaylee Goncalves, Madison Mogen, Xana Kernodle, and Ethan Chapin—were murdered inside their home near the university campus. Beginning on November 24, 2022, Ashley Guillard, a self-styled internet sleuth, posted numerous TikTok videos alleging that Rebecca Scofield, a professor at the university, ordered the murders because she was romantically involved with one of the victims. Scofield denied the allegations, and her attorney demanded that Guillard stop posting the videos. Guillard was defiant. "I'm not worried about Rebecca Scofield suing me because she will be using her resources to fight four murder cases," said Guillard.

On December 21, 2022, Scofield filed a defamation lawsuit against Guillard. "Professor Scofield has been damaged by Guillard's false statements," stated the lawsuit. "Her reputation has been tarnished, and she has suffered extreme emotional distress from the constant public attention and the ongoing online conversation discussing the false relationship with a student."

Scofield's lawyers anticipate that Guillard might be considered a public figure, so they allege that she acted with actual malice. The lawsuit states: "Guillard knew her statements were false because she had no knowledge about anything happening in Moscow, Idaho, or at the University of Idaho."

Quoted in *Rebecca Scofield v. Ashley Guillard*, Case 3:22-cv-00521, RFP December 21, 2022

While the Supreme Court has found that government officials cannot coerce private companies into suppressing speech, it remains to be seen whether the government can force private companies to publish content against their will. In 2021 Florida and Texas passed laws that prevent large social media websites from suppressing content based on political viewpoints, even if the companies find the content objectionable. Technology industry groups NetChoice and the Computer & Communications Industry Association filed lawsuits claiming that such laws violate the First Amendment, because they allow the government to dictate by law what content appears on social media platforms. In January 2023 the Supreme Court asked the Biden administration's Office of the Solicitor General, which oversees and conducts government cases before the Supreme Court, for its position on the state laws. If the high court hears a case regarding these laws, it may clarify questions regarding the role of social media as a forum for free speech.

> "Sometimes the right thing to do from a safety or security perspective isn't the best for privacy or free expression, so we have to choose what we believe is best for our community and for the world."[41]
>
> —Mark Zuckerberg, CEO of Meta

Regulating Hate Speech

Feeling bored during the COVID-19 pandemic in 2020, sixteen-year-old Payton Gendron began browsing the 4chan website. There he encountered various extremist ideas and conspiracy theories. Brazen in their outspokenness and forceful in their expression, these words challenged everything Gendron had learned at home and at school. The more he read, the more intrigued he became. A White male, Gendron was captivated by the White replacement theory, a racist doctrine that maintains that non-White minorities are replacing White majorities in the United States, Europe, and other countries with mostly White populations with the purpose of eliminating White culture. "I learned through infographics, [posts], and memes that the White race is dying out,"[42] Gendron later explained.

Inspired by Hate

His curiosity raging out of control, Gendron read the manifesto of Brenton Tarrant, a twenty-eight-year-old Australian man who subscribed to the White replacement theory. Acting on his beliefs, Tarrant went on a shooting rampage inside a mosque in Christchurch, New Zealand, and posted a live streamed video of the massacre. "Brenton's livestream started everything you see here," wrote Gendron in a 180-page manifesto that he posted online. "Without his livestream I would likely have no idea about the real problems the West is facing." Gendron also read about other racist mass shooters, including Patrick Crusius, Anders Breivik, Dylann Roof, and John Earnest. For two years, Gendron absorbed the hate-filled rants against minorities, slowly adopting the racist beliefs as his own. Gendron later said that in May 2022 he decided that he "would follow Tarrant's lead and the attacks of so many others like him."[43]

After posting his manifesto online, Gendron drove about 200 miles (322 km) from his home in Conklin, New York, to a Tops grocery store in Buffalo, because the location was known to have a high percentage of Black customers. Wearing body armor and armed with a military-style rifle, Gendron approached the market at about 2:30 p.m. According to police, Gendron opened fire on shoppers and store employees with his semiautomatic rifle while live streaming the attack on Twitch, a social media website. Within minutes, ten people lay dead. All ten were Black. In his manifesto, Gendron expressed his twisted, delusional thinking. "If we do rise up against the replacers, I expect that I will be let out [of prison] and honored amongst my people."[44]

This photo shows the Tops grocery store in Buffalo, New York, after a shooting killed ten people in 2022.

"You can't prevent people from being radicalized to violence, but we can address the relentless exploitation of the Internet to recruit and mobilize terrorism."[45]

—Joe Biden, forty-sixth US president

Stunned by the senseless loss of life, Americans across the country searched for ways to prevent future attacks. With gun ownership protected by the Second Amendment, attention turned to stopping violence at its source—the hate-filled calls to violence on the web. "You can't prevent people from being radicalized to violence, but we can address the relentless exploitation of the Internet to recruit and mobilize terrorism,"[45] said President Joe Biden at a memorial for the fallen held three days after the shooting in Buffalo.

Biden is not alone in thinking the government should do more to quell the spread of violent extremism online. Some experts believe the United States should follow the lead of many European nations and pass laws limiting hate speech. Following the Holocaust of the 1930s and 1940s, when Nazi Germany murdered 6 million Jews, Germany and other nations passed laws to curb the kind of racial and religious hatred that gave rise to the Holocaust. Many European laws limiting hate speech online have their roots in the Convention on Cybercrime of the Council of Europe, known as the Budapest Convention. This document defines hate speech as "all forms of expression which spread, incite, promote or justify racial hatred, xenophobia, anti-Semitism or other forms of hatred based on intolerance, including intolerance expressed by aggressive nationalism and ethnocentrism, discrimination and hostility against minorities, migrants and people of immigrant origin."[46]

Hate Speech and the First Amendment

Any law designed to suppress hate speech in the United States would have to be carefully worded to pass the legal challenges it would undoubtedly face. Under current law, speech that attacks people based on their race, religion, ethnic origin, or sexual orientation is protected by the First Amendment, unless it is expressed in a way that threatens individuals or immediately incites violence.

Two Supreme Court cases involving cross burning illustrate the fine line the court has drawn between the expression of an idea and the statement of a threat. In the first case, *R.A.V. v. St. Paul* (1992), the Supreme Court struck down a St. Paul, Minnesota, hate crime law because it made the expression of an idea a crime. The law called for special punishment for any person who "places on public or private property a symbol, object, appellation [name], characterization or graffiti, including, but not limited to, a burning cross or Nazi swastika, which one knows or has reasonable grounds to know arouses anger, alarm, or resentment in others on the basis of race, color, creed, religion, or gender."[47] Robert A. Viktora, the "R.A.V." in the case name, was convicted under this law because he burned a cross on the lawn of a Black family living in a mostly White neighborhood. The problem with the law was that

A Call for Criminalizing Hate Speech

Richard Stengel, a former editor of *Time* magazine, believes the United States should pass laws similar to the European laws that make hate speech a crime. He writes:

> The First Amendment protects the "thought that we hate," but it should not protect hateful speech that can cause violence by one group against another. In an age when everyone has a megaphone, that seems like a design flaw. . . .
>
> Domestic terrorists such as Dylann Roof and Omar Mateen and the El Paso shooter were consumers of hate speech. Speech doesn't pull the trigger, but does anyone seriously doubt that such hateful speech creates a climate where such acts are more likely? . . .
>
> Why shouldn't the states experiment with their own version of hate speech statutes to penalize speech that deliberately insults people based on religion, race, ethnicity and sexual orientation?
>
> All speech is not equal. And where truth cannot drive out lies, we must add new guardrails. I'm all for protecting "thought that we hate," but not speech that incites hate. It undermines the very values of a fair marketplace of ideas that the First Amendment is designed to protect.

Richard Stengel. "Why America Needs a Hate Speech Law." *Washington Post*, October 29

it criminalized speech against certain groups but not others. "The only interest . . . served by the content limitation is that of displaying the city council's special hostility towards the particular biases thus singled out. That is precisely what the First Amendment forbids,"[48] wrote Justice Antonin Scalia for the majority.

In *Virginia v. Black* (2003), the Supreme Court reviewed a Virginia law that makes it a felony "for any person . . . , with the intent of intimidating any person or group . . . , to burn a cross on the property of another, a highway or other public place."[49] Although the activity banned by the Virginia law was identical to the activity engaged in by Viktora, the high court found the Virginia law constitutional, because it applied to all cross burning that was meant to intimidate, not just to cross burning aimed at certain groups. Writing for the majority, Justice Sandra Day O'Connor explained:

> Unlike the statute at issue in *R. A. V.*, the Virginia statute does not single out for opprobrium only that speech directed toward "one of the specified disfavored topics." It does not matter whether an individual burns a cross with intent to intimidate because of the victim's race, gender, or religion, or because of the victim's "political affiliation, union membership, or homosexuality."[50]

"Instead of prohibiting all intimidating messages, Virginia may choose to regulate this subset of intimidating messages in light of cross burning's long and pernicious history as a signal of impending violence."[51]

—Sandra Day O'Connor, Supreme Court justice

The Virginia law also avoided the pitfall of trying to outlaw too many kinds of behavior at once. "Instead of prohibiting all intimidating messages, Virginia may choose to regulate this subset of intimidating messages in light of cross burning's long and pernicious history as a signal of impending violence,"[51] wrote O'Connor.

The court did strike down part of the law that said that any cross burning was, on its face (prima facie), evidence of the intent to intimidate. It was possible, the

People march in Washington, DC, in 2021, to protest hate crimes against Asian people in the United States. Researchers have found a correlation between hateful tweets and hate crimes.

court said, that the cross burning had another meaning, and juries must be allowed to consider such factors. O'Connor wrote:

> The act of burning a cross may mean that a person is engaging in constitutionally proscribable intimidation, or it may mean only that the person is engaged in core political speech. The prima facie evidence provision blurs the line between these meanings, ignoring all of the contextual factors that are necessary to decide whether a particular cross burning is intended to intimidate. The First Amendment does not permit such a shortcut.[52]

Incitement to Violence

The ruling in *Virginia v. Black* gives hope to those who wish to outlaw hate speech. It might be possible to craft a law that does not focus on particular victims but instead focuses on words that call for violence against anyone. As in *Virginia v. Black*, such a law would not outlaw all hate speech, only the hate speech designed to incite lawless action. Juries would have to decide whether the intent of the speech was to incite violence.

The Supreme Court's standard for the incitement of a crime is high, however. To be considered as incitement, the court wrote in *Brandenburg v. Ohio* (1969), speech must go beyond the "mere abstract teaching . . . of the moral propriety or even moral necessity for a resort to force and violence." The words must be aimed at "preparing a group for violent action and steeling it to such action."[53] Typically, such words are uttered in front of the persons being urged to violence.

Applying the *Brandenburg* standard of incitement to online speech would be difficult. However, the court might carve out another exception to the First Amendment that refers only to a narrow subclass of speech, as it did in *Virginia v. Black*. After all, *Brandenburg* was decided before the advent of the internet. Two New York University researchers, Rumi Chunara and Stephanie Cook, have found a correlation between online hate speech and physical violence. In 2019, Chunara and Cook used artificial intelligence to analyze 532 million tweets in one hundred cities across the United States. The researchers found that cities with the greatest number of targeted, hateful tweets also had the highest number of hate crimes. "Overall, our findings suggest that race/ethnicity–based online discrimination was associated with an increase in race/ethnicity–based hate crimes,"[54] write Chunara and Cook. Such scientific research supports the idea that online speech can have real-world consequences. Backed by scientific evidence linking hate speech and violence, Congress might be able to ban a narrow class of inciting speech without discriminating against particular viewpoints or ideas.

> "Our findings suggest that race/ethnicity–based online discrimination was associated with an increase in race/ethnicity–based hate crimes."[54]
>
> —Rumi Chunara and Stephanie Cook, researchers at New York University

A Circuit Court Judge Says Hate Speech Should Not Be Protected

On December 27, 2022, Judge Ronald Gould of the Ninth Circuit Court of Appeals issued a concurring opinion in *Chen v. Albany Unified School District* in which he called for tighter restrictions on hate speech. The case involved two students who were expelled from Albany High School in California for posting racist words and images on Instagram. The students sued the school district on First Amendment grounds. The Ninth Circuit Court of Appeals upheld the expulsion, citing the Supreme Court's decision in *Mahanoy Area School District v. B.L.* In his concurring opinion, Gould went even further:

> I write to stress that school officials, and government officials more broadly, should not be unduly constrained in their attempts to regulate hate speech for the purpose of protecting the intended targets of said speech. This may require some refining of the Supreme Court's prior guidance in its precedents. For example, while recognizing that my views on hate speech may be less protective of speech than some current doctrine, I would conclude here that the racist characterizations and images, dehumanizing African American students, is sufficient to show a threat of imminent violence, fights or other attacks on African Americans, including, within the school context, bullying and harassment.

Chen v. Albany Unified School District, D.C. No. 3:17-cv02478-JD (2022).

Social Media Companies Battle Hate Speech

Today most hate speech directed toward individuals occurs on social media platforms, not in person. According to Facebook, the occurrence of hate speech has skyrocketed in recent years. From April through June 2021, Facebook identified 31.5 million hate speech posts, an increase of 40 percent over the same three-month period in 2020 and an astounding 616% increase over the same period in 2019. In all, Facebook identified 96.4 million hate speech posts in 2021 alone. The social media giant identified 28.6 million hate speech posts in the first half of 2022, the most recent figures available. That number is down from the

ye ✓
@kanyewest

YE24 LOVE EVERYONE
#LOVESPEECH

This picture shows the tweet that caused musical artist Ye to be suspended from Twitter for violating the company's rule against inciting violence.

levels in 2021 but still represents a 236.4 percent increase from the same period in 2019.

Facebook removed the millions of incidents of hate speech, even if that speech would otherwise be protected by the First Amendment. The social media giant could do so because it is a private company and is permitted to set its own community standards and suppress content that violates those standards. YouTube, Instagram, and Twitter have similar community standards and similarly remove hate speech from their platforms. YouTube reported that it removed 90.4 percent of reported hate speech posts in 2021, up from 58.8 percent in 2020. Twitter took action against 1,126,990 different accounts from July through December 2020 for violating its hateful conduct policy—a 77 percent increase over the previous six-month period.

After Elon Musk took control of Twitter in October 2022 and announced that he would be reinstating many banned accounts, researchers at the Brookings Institution, Tufts University, and the Anti-Defamation League reported that the number of hate speech–containing tweets increased dramatically. "Elon Musk sent up the batsignal to every kind of racist, misogynist and homophobe that Twitter was open for business, and they have reacted accordingly,"[55] says Imran Ahmed, CEO of the Center for Countering Digital Hate.

Responding to a tweet by the *New York Times* that reported the researchers' findings and featured Ahmed's quote, Musk tweeted, "Utterly false."[56] In subsequent tweets, Musk said that the total number of impressions—the number of times hate speech tweets were seen—had declined by a third since he took over the company, dropping from 10 million in October to about 2.7 million in November. Much of this was due to new software that identified the automatic tweeting of bots. "Reducing the max allowed tweets/day to a number below what a speed typist on meth could do was helpful,"[57] Musk observed. In a highly visible move, Twitter suspended Ye (the musical artist formerly known as Kanye West) for sharing an image of a swastika in a Star of David. Musk tweeted that the suspension was for violating the company's "rule against incitement to violence."[58]

Despite the progress social media companies have made to limit hate speech, some experts are skeptical that technology can solve the problem. "Many excellent methods will be developed to improve the information environment, but the history of online systems shows that bad actors can and will always find ways around them,"[59] says Paul N. Edwards, a William J. Perry Fellow in International Security at Stanford University. Even if today's largest social media companies succeed in reducing hate speech, speakers with hateful messages can still use alternate social media platforms, websites like 4chan, encrypted message platforms like WhatsApp, and yet-to-be launched technologies to spread their verbal poison.

> "Many excellent methods will be developed to improve the information environment, but the history of online systems shows that bad actors can and will always find ways around them."[59]
>
> —Paul N. Edwards, William J. Perry Fellow in International Security at Stanford University

Although counterspeech has so far failed to drive hate speech from the marketplace of ideas, it offers the only real hope for ending the scourge of demeaning expression. Hate speech is false speech. Its fallacies must be exposed through education. Its lies must be confronted in discussion. And everyone must make a personal commitment to reject it whenever and wherever it appears.

The War on Government Leaks

On July 27, 2021, Daniel Hale, a former defense contractor at the National Geospatial-Intelligence Agency (NGA), stood before US district judge Liam O'Grady in a federal courtroom in Alexandria, Virginia. Five months earlier, Hale had pleaded guilty to violating the Espionage Act for sharing classified information with a journalist. While working for the NGA, Hale had printed thirty-six documents from his government computer, twenty-three of which were unrelated to his work at NGA. The documents detailed the use of military drones to kill enemy combatants far from the battlefield in Afghanistan, strikes that often killed civilians as well. The documents revealed that during one five-month period, nearly 90 percent of the people killed were not the intended targets. Hale gave at least seventeen of the twenty-three documents to the online publication the Intercept, which published the documents in whole or in part. Eleven of the published documents were marked as top secret or secret.

Putting Conscience Above the Law

Seeking leniency from the court, Hale explained his actions. "I believe that it is wrong to kill, but it is especially wrong to kill the defenseless,"[60] Hale told O'Grady. "I am here because I stole something that was never mine to take—precious human life. I couldn't keep living in a world in which people pretend that things weren't happening that were. Please, your honor, forgive me for taking papers instead of human lives."[61]

O'Grady acknowledged Hale's humanitarian motives but said he went about his protest the wrong way. "You are not being prosecuted for speaking out about the drone program killing innocent people," O'Grady said. "You could have been a whistleblower ... without taking any of these documents."[62] The judge then sentenced Hale to forty-five months in prison.

After the sentencing, Betsy Reed, editor in chief of the Intercept, defended Hale's actions. "These documents revealed the truth about the US government's secretive, murderous drone war, including that the killing of civilians was far more widespread than previously acknowledged," Reed declared. Stating that the Intercept does not disclose its sources, Reed would not refer to Hale by name, but she still lauded his actions: "Whoever brought the documents in question to light undoubtedly served a noble public purpose."[63]

Prior to Hale's trial, his attorneys argued that the case should be dismissed because by punishing Hale, the government was suppressing freedom of the press. They argued that the law Hale was charged with breaking—the Espionage Act of 1917—was

This picture shows a military drone. In 2021, Daniel Hale shared classified documents showing that US military drone strikes in Afghanistan often killed civilians as well as enemy combatants.

designed to punish spies, not journalists or whistleblowers. Instead, they wrote, the law is now being "used regularly against those who leak for no purpose other than informing their fellow citizens about their own government." This use of the law, they argued, violates the First Amendment. "It is indisputable that this prosecution treads closely to freedoms that are essential to a free and democratic society,"[64] Hale's lawyers wrote.

The government responded to these claims by pointing out that Hale had signed several nondisclosure agreements as a condition of being granted access to classified information. Because of these agreements, Hale knew that sharing the secret documents with unauthorized people was against the law. The government's lawyers cited a decision by the circuit court of appeals to show that the First Amendment did not shield Hale's actions. "Those who accept positions of trust involving a duty not to disclose information they lawfully acquire while performing their responsibilities have no First Amendment right to disclose that information,"[65] stated the court. Siding with the government, O'Grady did not dismiss the case on constitutional grounds, allowing it to go to trial.

Compelling Interest

The denial of Hale's First Amendment claims is an example of one of the most important exceptions to freedom of speech; namely, when a compelling interest of the government permits the suppression or punishment of expression. The logic behind the compelling interest doctrine is simple. People are born with basic rights, but those rights are "very uncertain and constantly exposed to the invasion of others,"[66] as the English philosopher John Locke pointed out in his *Second Treatise of Government*. The only way to secure individual rights is to establish the rule of law through a government. Such a government must be strong and effective if it is to protect individual rights. That is why the ability of the government to survive and function supersedes all other competing values and interests, including the right of free speech.

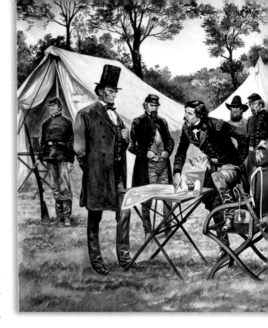

This piece of artwork depicts Abraham Lincoln planning a campaign during the American Civil War. During the war, Lincoln made a compelling argument for the limitation of some types of free speech.

One of the clearest compelling interest arguments ever made came from President Abraham Lincoln during the Civil War. Lincoln pointed out that because of the rebellion by the South, the laws of the United States were "failing of execution, in nearly one-third of the states." Lincoln, who had ordered the censorship of telegraph messages, prohibited the printing of war news without governmental approval, and closed newspapers critical of his policies, argued that the nation's laws should not be allowed to fail everywhere just to protect one right or one law, including the First Amendment. "Are all the laws, but one, to go unexecuted, and the government itself go to pieces, lest that one be violated?"[67] Lincoln asked. For him, the answer was obvious: the government must preserve itself first, if it is to preserve the rights the Constitution guarantees.

The compelling interest of government extends to many areas: protecting the government from rebellion within, defending itself from enemies abroad, collecting taxes necessary for its operation, and many other activities. The government, wrote Justice Joseph Bradley in *Legal Tender Cases* (1870), "is invested with all those inherent and implied powers which, at the time of adopting the Constitution, were generally considered to belong to every government as such, and as being essential to the exercise of its functions."[68]

Strict Scrutiny

As sweeping as the compelling interest doctrine is, it does not mean that all government activities outweigh the right to free

In September 2020 the Ninth Circuit Court of Appeals ruled that a mass domestic surveillance program conducted by the National Security Agency (NSA) was illegal and possibly unconstitutional. In the same ruling, however, the court declared that the man who brought the program to light by leaking secret documents about it to the press could still stand trial for violating the Espionage Act of 1917.

Edward Snowden, a former computer intelligence consultant who worked for the NSA, allegedly stole 1.7 million classified documents from the NSA and leaked 200,000 of them to journalists in 2013. The documents revealed that the NSA had collected millions of Americans' telephone records without any kind of warrant, a violation of the Foreign Intelligence Surveillance Act. Snowden fled to Russia to avoid prosecution, and in September 2022 he received Russian citizenship.

The American Civil Liberties Union, which helped bring the case to appeal, applauded the verdict. "Today's ruling is a victory for our privacy rights," stated the organization, adding that the ruling "makes plain that the NSA's bulk collection of Americans' phone records violated the Constitution." In keeping with other precedents, the news outlets that published the stolen documents were not charged with any crimes.

Quoted in Raphael Satter, "U.S. Court: Mass Surveillance Program Exposed by Snowden Was Illegal," Reuters, September 2, 2020. www.reuters.com.

speech. On the contrary, very few do. Government restrictions on free speech must pass what is known as the strict scrutiny test. David L. Hudson Jr., a law professor at Belmont University, writes:

> Strict scrutiny is the highest form of judicial review that courts use to evaluate the constitutionality of laws, regulations or other governmental policies under legal challenge. . . . Under a strict scrutiny analysis, a law that restricts freedom of speech must achieve a compelling government interest and be narrowly tailored to that interest or be the least speech-restrictive means available to the government.[69]

If there is a way for the government to achieve its goals without suppressing free speech, it is required to do so. It can only violate the First Amendment as a last resort.

The government has failed to meet the strict scrutiny test in many free speech cases, including ones involving national security. In one of the most famous cases, known as the Pentagon Papers case, a former defense analyst named Daniel Ellsberg gave a secret report he had helped write to the *New York Times* and the *Washington Post* as part of his efforts to help end the Vietnam War. The report, officially titled "History of U.S. Decision-Making in Vietnam, 1945–68," described events that led to American involvement in Vietnam.

The *New York Times* published the first of nine planned installments of the report on June 13, 1971, and the *Washington Post* began publishing the documents five days later. The government, which had classified these documents as secret, argued that their publication would prolong the war and endanger lives. Based on this compelling interest, the US district courts in New York City and Washington, DC, issued injunctions, barring the newspapers from publishing more of the stolen information.

Two federal appeals courts split on whether the injunctions were constitutional, so the Supreme Court heard the two cases together on June 26, 1971. Four days later, the high court gave its ruling. It struck down the injunctions, stating that the government did not meet the "heavy burden of showing justification for the imposition of such restraint." The court pointed out that the period covered by the documents had ended three years earlier, in 1968. Although embarrassing to the government, the material in the Pentagon Papers did not appear to be especially timely or sensitive. Concurring with the decision, Justice Hugo Black wrote, "The press was protected so that it could bare the secrets of government and inform the people. . . . Far from deserving condemnation for their courageous reporting, *The New York Times*, *The Washington Post* and other newspapers should be commended for serving the purpose that the Founding Fathers saw so clearly."[70]

> "The press was protected so that it could bare the secrets of government and inform the people."[70]
>
> —Hugo Black, Supreme Court justice

Seeking to Punish Publishers

The compelling interest doctrine has been used with greater effect against leakers of secret documents than with publishers of them. For example, in 2013 the government successfully prosecuted military intelligence analyst Chelsea Manning (then known as Bradley Manning) for providing thousands of sensitive military documents—some classified and some unclassified—to the online publisher WikiLeaks. Manning was sentenced to thirty-five years at the US Disciplinary Barracks at Fort Leavenworth. In 2017 President Barack Obama commuted Manning's sentence to the time she had served since her arrest in 2010.

The government also indicted the founder of WikiLeaks, Julian Assange, on seventeen charges of espionage and one charge of computer misuse for "aiding, abetting, and causing" Manning to provide him with the classified documents and for publishing the documents on WikiLeaks. "Assange's actions risked serious harm to United States national security to the benefit of our adversar-

In 2022, protesters in London hold up a banner supporting WikiLeaks founder Julian Assange. The US government indicted Assange for espionage; however, some free speech advocates disagree with this label.

When Julian Assange was indicted under the Espionage Act for publishing classified documents, the editorial board of the *New York Times* denounced the government's action:

> Invoking the Espionage Act in this case threatens to blur the distinction between a journalist exposing government malfeasance—something that news organizations do with regularity—and foreign spies seeking to undermine the nation's security. . . .
>
> The new indictment . . . is a marked escalation in the effort to prosecute Mr. Assange, one that could have a chilling effect on American journalism as it has been practiced for generations. It is aimed straight at the heart of the First Amendment.
>
> The new charges focus on receiving and publishing classified material from a government source. That is something journalists do all the time. They did it with the Pentagon Papers and in countless other cases where the public benefited from learning what was going on behind closed doors, even though the sources may have acted illegally. This is what the First Amendment is designed to protect: the ability of publishers to provide the public with the truth.

Editorial Board, "Julian Assange's Indictment Aims at the Heart of the First Amendment," *New York Times*, May 23, 2019. www.nytimes.com.

ies,"[71] said the US Department of Justice. The charges carry a maximum sentence of 175 years in prison.

Free speech advocates question the prosecution of Assange, less for the fourteen charges that involve obtaining the stolen documents and more for the three charges that involve publishing them. Gabe Rottman of the Reporters Committee for Freedom of the Press writes:

> Counts 15 through 17 of the . . . Assange indictment represent the first time a grand jury has issued an indictment based on a pure publication theory. . . . The Justice Department now seeks to punish the pure act of publication of newsworthy government secrets under the nation's spying laws. . . . This goes beyond just a threat to sources or newsgathering; it's a direct threat to news reporting.[72]

> "Freedom of expression is the well-spring of our civilization— the civilization we seek to protect and maintain and further by recognizing the right of Congress to put some limitation upon expression. Such are the paradoxes of life."[73]
>
> —Felix Frankfurter, Supreme Court justice

After years of being given sanctuary in the Ecuadorean embassy in London, Assange was arrested and put in jail in London for unrelated charges. As of early 2023, he was fighting an extradition request from the United States. His lawyers say he is being prosecuted and punished for his political opinions—which is grounds under British law for blocking extradition.

According to the doctrine of compelling interest, freedom of speech and censorship can—and must—coexist. Without a free exchange of ideas, society will stagnate and die. But without some limits on speech, the survival of the government would be at risk, imperiling all the rights it protects. Perhaps Justice Felix Frankfurter put it best in his concurring opinion in *Dennis v. United States* (1951): "Freedom of expression is the well-spring of our civilization—the civilization we seek to protect and maintain and further by recognizing the right of Congress to put some limitation upon expression. Such are the paradoxes of life."[73]

Introduction: Meeting the Challenge of Toxic Expression

1. Chen v. Albany Unified School District, D.C. No. 3:17-cv02478-JD (2022).
2. Quoted in University of Birmingham, "'Fake News' Poses Corrosive Existential Threat to Democracy," July 27, 2022. www.birmingham.ac.uk.
3. United States v. Alvarez, 567 U.S. 709 (2012).
4. United States v. Alvarez.
5. David Pozen, "'Truth Drives Out Lies' and Other Misinformation," Knight First Amendment Institute, February 9, 2022. https://knightcolumbia.org.

Chapter One: The Doctrine of Free Speech

6. Quoted in Vanessa Serna, "'It's a Social Credit System': Stanford Professor Revealed to Be Blacklisted by Twitter for Opposing COVID Lockdowns Says It's like McCarthyism of 1950s Because Woke Execs Disliked His 'Dangerous' Ideas," *Daily Mail* (London), December 11, 2022. www.dailymail.co.uk.
7. Elon Musk (@elonmusk), "Dear Twitter Advertisers," Twitter, October 27, 2022, 6:08 a.m. https://twitter.com/elonmusk/status/1585619322239561728.
8. Whitney v. California, 274 U.S. 357 (1927).
9. John Milton, *Areopagitica.* Saylor Academy, 2012. www.saylor.org.
10. Milton, *Areopagitica.*
11. Quoted in J.W. Ehrlich, ed., *Ehrlich's Blackstone*. San Carlos, CA: Nourse, 1959, p. 813.
12. Dennis v. United States, 341 U.S. 494 (1951).
13. New York Times Co. v. United States, 403 U.S. 713 (1971).
14. Smith v. California, 361 U.S. 147 (1959).
15. Robertson v. Baldwin, 165 U.S. 275 (1897).
16. Abrams v. United States, 250 U.S. 616 (1919).
17. United States v. Rumely, 345 U.S. 41 (1953).
18. David Schultz, "Marketplace of Ideas," First Amendment Encyclopedia, June 2017. https://mtsu.edu.
19. Reed v. Town of Gilbert, 576 U.S. ___ (2015).
20. Richard Stengel, "Why America Needs a Hate Speech Law," *Washington Post*, October 29, 2019. www.washingtonpost.com.
21. Elon Musk (@elonmusk), "By 'free speech,' I simply mean that which matches the law," Twitter, April 26, 2022, 12:33 p.m. https://twitter.com/elonmusk/status/1519036983137509376.

Chapter Two: Free Speech on Campus

22. Quoted in Michel Martin, "A Recent Skirmish over Free Speech Involved High School Students and Their Adviser," *All Things Considered*, NPR, September 18, 2022. www.npr.org.
23. Tinker v. Des Moines Independent Community School District, 393 U.S. 503 (1969).
24. Tinker v. Des Moines Independent Community School District.

25. Quoted in CBS News, "Oregon Student Disciplined for 'Trump Border Wall' T-shirt to get $25,000," July 25, 2018. www.cbsnews.com.

26. Quoted in Douglas Ernst, "Addison Barnes Victorious: Judge's Ruling Allows Student to Wear Pro-Trump 'Border Wall' Shirt," *Washington Times*, June 1, 2018. www.washingtontimes.com.

27. Morse v. Frederick, 551 U.S. 393 (2007).

28. Morse v. Frederick.

29. Morse v. Frederick.

30. Mahanoy Area School District v. B.L., 594 U.S. ___ (2021).

31. Mahanoy Area School District v. B.L.

Chapter Three: False and Misleading Information

32. Jack Brewster et al., "Beware the 'New Google:' TikTok's Search Engine Pumps Toxic Misinformation to Its Young Users," Misinformation Monitor, September 2022. www.newsguardtech.com.

33. Brewster et al., "Beware the 'New Google.'"

34. New York Times Co. v. Sullivan, 376 U.S. 254 (1964).

35. Cantwell v. State of Connecticut, 310 U.S. 296 (1940).

36. New York Times Co. v. Sullivan.

37. Rosenblatt v. Baer, 383 U.S. 75 (1966).

38. Quoted in David Zweig (@davidzweig), "12. Culbertson wrote that the Biden team was 'very angry' that Twitter had not been more aggressive in deplatforming multiple accounts," Twitter, December 26, 2022, 9:32 a.m. https://twitter.com/davidzweig/status/1607383819287515137.

39. Elon Musk (@elonmusk), "If this isn't a violation of the Constitution's First Amendment, what is?" Twitter, December 2, 2022, 5:24 p.m. https://twitter.com/elonmusk/status/1598850682487943168.

40. Bantam Books, Inc. v. Sullivan, 372 U.S. 58 (1963).

41. Quoted in Lauren Feiner, "Mark Zuckerberg and Jack Dorsey Testify Before the Senate Tuesday," CNBC, November 17, 2020. www.cnbc.com.

Chapter Four: Regulating Hate Speech

42. Quoted in Vivek Saxena, "'Extreme' Buffalo Gunman Threatened HS Graduation Shooting, Referred for 'Mental Health Eval,'" BPR, May 15, 2022. www.bizpacreview.com.

43. Quoted in Bridget Johnson, "10 Killed in Buffalo Supermarket Attack Allegedly Inspired by Christchurch Terrorist Manifesto," Homeland Security Today, May 14, 2022. www.hstoday.us.

44. Quoted in Johnson, "10 Killed in Buffalo Supermarket Attack Allegedly Inspired by Christchurch Terrorist Manifesto."

45. Quoted in White House, "Remarks by President Biden and First Lady Biden Honoring the Lives Lost in Buffalo, New York, and Calling on All Americans to Condemn White Supremacy," May 17, 2022. www.whitehouse.gov.

46. Quoted in British Institute of Human Rights, *Mapping Study on Projects Against Hate Speech Online*. Strasbourg: Council of Europe, 2012, p. 8.

47. R.A.V. v. City of St. Paul, 505 U.S. 377 (1992).

48. R.A.V. v. City of St. Paul.

49. Virginia v. Black, 538 U.S. 343 (2003).

50. Virginia v. Black.

51. Virginia v. Black.

52. Virginia v. Black.

53. Brandenburg v. Ohio, 395 U.S. 444 (1969).

54. Quoted in New York University Tandon School of Engineering, "Hate Speech on Twitter Predicts Frequency of Real-Life Hate Crimes," June 24, 2019. https://engineering.nyu.edu.

55. Quoted in Mia Sato, "Hate Speech Is Soaring on Twitter Under Elon Musk, Report Finds," The Verge, December 2, 2022. www.theverge.com.

56. Elon Musk (@elonmusk), "Utterly false," Twitter, December 2, 2022, 11:07 a.m. https://twitter.com/elonmusk/status/1598755659499044879.

57. Elon Musk (@elonmusk), "Reducing the max allowed tweets/day to a number below what a speed typist on meth could do was helpful," Twitter, November 23, 2022, 9:39 p.m. https://twitter.com/elonmusk/status/1595653241605591041.

58. Elon Musk (@elonmusk), "I tried my best," Twitter, December 1, 2022, 9:04 p.m. https://twitter.com/elonmusk/status/1598543670990495744.

59. Quoted in Janna Anderson and Lee Rainie, "The Future of Truth and Misinformation Online," Pew Research Center, October 19, 2017. www.pewresearch.org.

Chapter Five: The War on Government Leaks

60. Quoted in Rachel Weiner, "Daniel Hale, Who Leaked Information on U.S. Drone Warfare, Sentenced to 45 Months in Prison," *Washington Post*, July 27, 2021. www.washingtonpost.com.

61. Quoted in Ryan Devereaux and Murtaza Hussain, "Daniel Hale Sentenced to 45 Months in Prison for Drone Leak," The Intercept, July 27, 2021. https://theintercept.com.

62. Quoted in Weiner, "Daniel Hale, Who Leaked Information on U.S. Drone Warfare, Sentenced to 45 Months in Prison."

63. Quoted in Devereaux and Hussain, "Daniel Hale Sentenced to 45 Months in Prison for Drone Leak."

64. Quoted in Matthew Barakat, "Lawyers Say Leaks Prosecution Violates Freedom of the Press," Associated Press, September 16, 2019. https://apnews.com.

65. John A. Boehner, Appellee v. James A. Mcdermott, Appellant, 484 F.3d 573 (D.C. Cir. 2007).

66. John Locke, *Second Treatise of Government*. New York: Barnes & Noble, 2004, p. 73.

67. Quoted in Michael Kent Curtis, *Free Speech, "the People's Darling Privilege": Struggles for Freedom of Expression in American History*. Durham, NC: Duke University Press, 2000, p. 306.

68. Legal Tender Cases, 79 U.S. 457 (1870).

69. David L. Hudson Jr., "Strict Scrutiny," First Amendment Encyclopedia, August 16, 2021. https://mtsu.edu.

70. New York Times Co. v. United States.

71. US Department of Justice, "WikiLeaks Founder Julian Assange Charged in 18-Count Superseding Indictment," May 23, 2019. www.justice.gov.

72. Gabe Rottman, "The Assange Indictment Seeks to Punish Pure Publication," *Lawfare* (blog), May 24, 2019. www.lawfareblog.com.

73. Dennis v. United States.

American Civil Liberties Union (ACLU)

www.aclu.org

The ACLU is a national organization that works to defend Americans' civil liberties as guaranteed by the US Constitution. It opposes all forms of censorship and seeks to protect the rights of free speech and a free press.

American Library Association (ALA)

www.ala.org

The ALA provides leadership for the development, promotion, and improvement of library and information services and the profession of librarianship to enhance learning and ensure access to information for all. Its website includes a section titled "Fight Censorship."

Center for Democracy & Technology (CDT)

https://cdt.org

The CDT works to preserve the user-controlled nature of the internet and champion freedom of expression. It supports laws, corporate policies, and technology tools that protect the privacy of internet users and that advocate for stronger legal controls on government surveillance.

Constitutional Rights Foundation (CRF)

www.crf-usa.org

The CRF is a nonprofit, nonpartisan, community-based organization dedicated to instilling in American youth a deeper understanding of citizenship through values expressed in the Constitution and its Bill of Rights and to educating them to become active and responsible participants in society.

Electronic Frontier Foundation (EFF)

www.eff.org

Founded in 1990, the EFF works to ensure that the civil liberties guaranteed in the Constitution and the Bill of Rights are applied to cutting-edge communication technologies. The EFF enlists the help of lawyers, policy analysts, activists, and technologists to advocate on behalf of consumers, innovators, coders, and others.

FactCheck.org

www.factcheck.org

FactCheck.org is a nonprofit website with the self-described mission of reducing the level of deception and confusion in US politics. The website features a "Viral Spiral" section devoted to debunking misinformation.

National Coalition Against Censorship (NCAC)

https://ncac.org

The NCAC opposes censorship in any form, believing it to be against the First Amendment right to freedom of speech. It works to educate the public about the dangers of censorship, including censorship of violence on television and in movies and music.

PEN American Center

https://pen.org

The center is the American branch of a worldwide organization of poets and playwrights, editors and essayists, and novelists—PEN for short. Its Freedom to Write Committee organizes letter-writing campaigns on behalf of writers around the globe who are censored or imprisoned. The organization publishes a biweekly *Free Expression* newsletter and a monthly *Educational Censorship* newsletter.

Snopes

www.snopes.com

Founded in 1994, Snopes is a leading fact-checking website. Its easily searchable database allows users to see what the Snopes investigators have learned about various social media posts and other online stories. Its fact-check articles often include links to documenting sources so readers can do independent research and make up their own minds.

Books

Dennis Baron, *You Can't Always Say What You Want*. New York: Cambridge University Press, 2023.

Alan Dershowitz, *The Case Against the New Censorship*. New York: Hot Books, 2021.

Kathryn Hulick, *Thinking Critically: Fake News*. San Diego, CA: ReferencePoint, 2020.

Meryl Loonin, *Banned Books: The Controversy over What Students Read*. San Diego, CA: ReferencePoint, 2023.

Cailin O'Connor and James Owen Weatherall, *The Misinformation Age: How False Beliefs Spread*. New Haven, CT: Yale University Press, 2020.

Thomas Rid, *Active Measures: The Secret History of Disinformation and Political Warfare*. New York: Farrar, Straus & Giroux, 2020.

Ian Rosenberg, *The Fight for Free Speech: Ten Cases That Define Our First Amendment*. New York: NYU Press, 2023.

Internet Sources

Thomas A. Berry, "Courts Should Take 'Jawboning' Claims Seriously," Cato Institute, December 7, 2022. www.cato.org.

Connor Brownfield, "The 11 Largest National Security Leaks in American History," *Saturday Evening Post*, September 13, 2022. www.saturday eveningpost.com.

Freedom Forum Institute, "Freedom of Speech FAQ," 2023. www .freedomforuminstitute.org.

Farhad Manjoo, "I Spoke to a Scholar of Conspiracy Theories and I'm Scared for Us," *New York Times*, October 21, 2020. www.nytimes.com.

David French, "Elon Musk and Tucker Carlson Don't Understand the First Amendment," *The Atlantic*, December 3, 2022. www.theatlantic.com.

Foundation for Individual Rights and Expression, "Free Speech in High School," 2022. www.thefire.org.

Jeffrey Rosen, "Elon Musk Is Right That Twitter Should Follow the First Amendment," *The Atlantic*, May 2, 2022. www.theatlantic.com.